HISTORIC
COMMUNITIES

Home Crafts

Bobbie Kalman

Crabtree Publishing Company
www.Crabtreebooks.com

Toronto · Oxford · New York

HISTORIC COMMUNITIES

Created by Bobbie Kalman

For my Aunt Marika

Editors
Christine Arthurs
Marni Hoogeveen

Design
Heather Delfino

Pasteup
Adriana Longo

Published by
Crabtree Publishing Company

PMB 16A
350 Fifth Avenue   612 Welland Ave.,   73 Lime Walk
Suite 3308   St. Catharines,   Headington
New York   Ontario, Canada   Oxford OX3 7AD
N.Y. 10118   L2M 5V6   United Kingdom

Cataloguing in Publication Data

Kalman, Bobbie, 1947-
    Home crafts

(Historic communities)
Includes index.
ISBN 0-86505-485-1 (library bound) ISBN 0-86505-505-X (pbk.)
A wide variety of home crafts are examined, including spinning
and weaving, soap and candle making, and quilting.

1. Handicraft - Juvenile literature. 2. Frontier and pioneer life -
Juvenile literature. I. Title. II. Series: Kalman, Bobbie, 1947-
Historic communities.

TT160.K26 1993   j745.5 20

LC 93-6218

Contents

What is a craft?

When we talk about **crafts** today, we usually mean making things for fun. You have probably made crafts in art class at school. In this case, a craft is a handmade work of art. The word craft has another meaning. It is also a **trade** or occupation that requires skill. Both meanings can be used when we talk about the crafts in this book.

A different way of life

The settlers who came to North America found that their lives were very difficult just after they arrived. Many had lived in towns or cities where household goods had been made for them. They could go to stores and buy ready-made items such as material, clothes, soap, and candles. In their new land, on the other hand, there were no stores or workshops nearby.

Made in the home

Everything the settlers used to buy before, now had to be made in the home. All kinds of useful objects were carved from wood, woven out of straw, and sewn from leather by the settlers. They made candles and soap, quilts and rugs.

Artisans of the home

Women worked very hard to make all the household things their families needed. Spinning, weaving, and sewing were just some of the skills they had to learn in order to provide clothes for everyone. Because of their special skills, we can call settler women the craftspeople, or **artisans**, of the home.

For settlers, making crafts was part of everyday life. Women and children made all kinds of useful household items such as candles and baskets, and professional craftspeople provided goods such as pottery.

Clothes from scratch

The wooly fleece of a sheep kept the animal warm all winter. In spring, it was sheared off and made into clothes to keep the settlers warm.

Some people make their own clothes. They buy a pattern and cloth and use an electric sewing machine to sew the garment. When the settlers made clothes, they first had to weave cloth from raw materials such as wool or flax.

Wool from sheep

Clothes made from woolen cloth came from the coats of sheep. Sheep grew thick coverings of **fleece** during the winter months. The settlers **sheared** off this fleece in spring when the animals no longer needed it. The pile of fleece had to be washed, greased, carded, spun, dyed, and woven into cloth before it was ready to be sewn into clothes.

Washing and carding

As they were grazing, sheep picked up all kinds of dirt on their coats. Burrs, sticks, and mud were matted into the fleece. The cut wool had to be washed to be cleansed of all these things. Afterwards, it was greased because its natural oils were lost in washing. The wool was then ready to be **carded**. Carding was done with two paddles, each of which had wire teeth on one side. Carding mixed and fluffed the wool.

*Wool was mixed and fluffed between two paddles called **cards** (above). Perhaps the girl below, with the help of her mother, made the shawl she is wearing from a pile of wool such as the one behind her.*

Spinning required a skilled hand. A spinster had to stand while using a giant "monster" spinning wheel such as the one shown below.

Spinning

After carding, the clean bunches of fleece were ready to be spun into long strands of **yarn** on a spinning wheel. The act of spinning stretches and twists fibers of wool in such a way that they cannot come apart. Spinning wheels twisted the wool evenly and kept the yarn spinning at a steady rate. The spinster kept the wheel moving with her foot and held the wool tightly between her fingers. She had to hold it at just the right angle to keep it from bunching.

Wool was sometimes spun on big "monster wheels," which were operated from a standing position. The spinster walked three steps forward and then three steps back.

Dyeing

The settlers used some wool in its natural color, but they liked colorful dyed wool, too. Dyes are used to change the color of wool into many lovely shades. The settlers made dyes from natural ingredients such as bark and roots. Flowers and berries were also good sources of color. For instance, dandelions made a dark yellow dye, and cranberries were used to dye things red.

The settlers made dyes by drying out special parts of plants, crushing them with a **mortar** and **pestle**, and boiling the powder in water. The wool was dyed either before or after it was woven by dipping it into large pots of boiling colored water.

To produce an even color, this settler (above) dyes wool before she spins it. Imaginative settlers created all sorts of colors from natural ingredients (below).

9

The hackle was used to straighten strands of linen, leaving long, silky threads.

A flax plant

Linen from flax

Linen is a material made from a plant called flax. It was used to make treasured items such as sheets, tablecloths, napkins, towels, and clothing. People were especially proud of their fine linen shirts. Flax fibers were spun, dyed, and woven, just as wool was, but preparing these fibers was much more difficult.

After the flax plants were harvested, the stalks were pulled through a **ripple**, a coarse wooden comb, which removed the seeds. They were soaked and broken into short pieces with a wooden crusher. The fibers were then combed straight on a **hackle**. Only the fine, silky strands known as **line** remained. These were spun on a small spinning wheel and woven into cloth called **linen**.

Light and bright cotton

The settlers who lived in northern areas bought cloth made from cotton at the general store. It was expensive, but settlers still preferred it in summer because it was much cooler to wear than either wool or linen.

Cotton grows on cotton plants in the south. Cotton plants have yellow blossoms that wither and die and become sticky green capsules called **bolls**. The bolls turn brown and burst open in the fall, revealing black seeds and white cotton fibers.

The seeds were separated from the fibers in a process called **ginning**. The remaining fibers were carded in much the same way that wool was carded. The result of spinning was a thin thread, which was woven into cloth and dyed.

The settlers who did not live in the south, where cotton grows, bought cotton fabric at the general store.

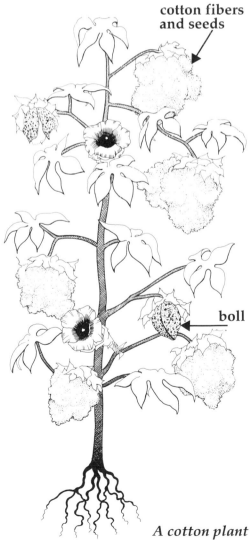

cotton fibers and seeds

boll

A cotton plant

11

Weaving

Wool, linen, and cotton were all woven in the same way. In the early days, weaving was done on homemade **hand looms**. Linen was made into summer clothing, napkins, and sheets. Wool was woven into blankets and warm winter clothes. When wool and linen were woven together, the fabric was called **linsey-woolsey**.

Warp and weft

Weaving is meshing together threads that run in two different directions. The lengthwise threads are called the **warp**; those running crosswise are the **weft**. If you look at a piece of linen under a magnifying glass, you will see these threads. The weaver threw a **shuttle**, which carried the weft

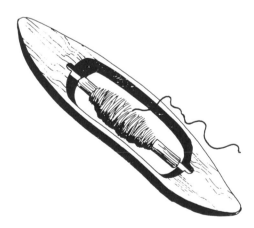

A loom shuttle

A loom was a valued piece of equipment. Without a loom, settlers could not weave cloth for making clothes.

threads back and forth between the warp threads. After each toss of the shuttle, the weaver used the **beater** to push the weft thread against the already-woven material to form a flat, smooth piece of cloth. Weaving took a long time, so the settlers welcomed the arrival of professional weavers to their villages. They then took wool or flax to the weaving shop to have cloth made.

Not just a "woman's" job

Although women did most of the carding and spinning, men as well as women did the work of weaving. Sometimes men who knew how to weave earned a living by traveling around the country-side, weaving cloth for many different families.

A weaver (top) examines the threads on his hand loom to make sure everything is working properly. By using different colored threads, weavers created patterns in their cloth such as the one shown above.

(above) The tricky task of making delicate lace produced beautiful results. Lace-trimmed tablecloths, sheets, and clothing were very popular in settler times.

(right) One way to make a carpet was to pull pieces of yarn through backing made of heavy burlap and tie them with a special needle. This was called rug hooking.

Busy needles

All kinds of beautiful and useful things for the home were made with different kinds of needles. Sewing, rug hooking, making lace, and crocheting were just some of the settler needle crafts. Of all the needle crafts, knitting was the most important one. The settlers knitted woolen socks, mitts, scarves, sweaters, and long underwear to keep out the winter cold. Blankets, chair covers, and curtains were also knitted.

Embroidered squares such as the one shown above were called samplers because children stitched them using samples of all the basic embroidery stitches.

(left) A selection of just a few crafts that can be made using needles

Learning to write with a needle

How did you learn your ABCs? In earlier times, young children learned the two skills of sewing and writing by making **samplers**. A sampler was a piece of linen on which the letters of the alphabet, numbers from one to ten, and a few simple pictures were drawn. Children practiced their letters and numbers while learning how to make basic embroidery stitches at the same time. After finishing this first simple sampler, they often sewed Bible verses on a second one.

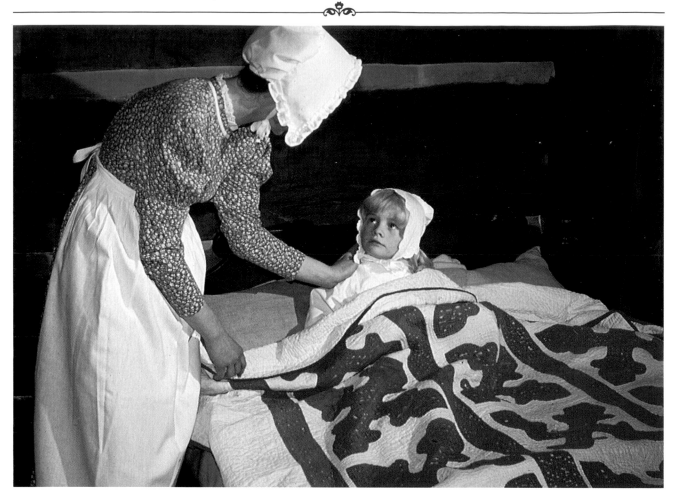

Quilts, useful works of art

Perhaps you have seen a quilt that was made a long time ago. Today antique quilts are treasured by their owners and passed down from generation to generation. These original and useful works of art took a long time to make because they each contain thousands of tiny stitches that were all sewn by hand. Does your family own a quilt?

Colorful quilts kept the settlers warm because they had three layers that trapped in heat and kept out the cold. The bottom sheet was plain, and the middle layer was a thick material called **stuffing**. The top layer had lovely patterns.

Settler homes did not have furnaces for heating, so people kept warm under cosy quilts.

16

Patterned patches

A quilt started out as a number of small squares. Each square was made from scraps of colored material, which were sewn to form a picture or pattern. When there were enough patches, the squares were all stitched together into a large sheet.

Popular designs

Girls and women used their imaginations to create beautiful quilts. Some quilters used popular designs such as "log cabin," "flower basket," and "double-link chain." Other women created their own designs, some of which told about their lives in pictures. Young settler women made at least two quilts each before they got married.

Quilts were made in all sorts of patterns and designs. No two were identical because they were all handmade.

After all three layers of a quilt were made, settler women held quilting bees (above) to sew them together. These gatherings were times of fun and friendship.

(right) There were many steps involved in making the top layer of a quilt. First, all the scraps had to be arranged in a pattern. After the small patches were made, they were then stitched together.

A quilting bee

Whenever settlers got together to do work, the event was called a **bee**. At a quilting bee, several women gathered to help stitch a quilt. The three layers of the quilt were stretched over a huge table-like frame so the quilters could reach each section more easily. The quilt was rolled up on the frame as each section was completed. Even with extra hands, the job could take a whole day.

A test of strength

Completing a quilt was a happy event that was usually followed by a party. After the work was finished, the men joined the women for a meal and dancing. Sometimes the young settlers played kissing games or tested the strength of the quilt by tossing a young man in the air and catching him in the finely stitched cover.

Make a patchwork quilt

You can make a patchwork quilt at your school. Suggest the idea to your teacher, librarian, or principal. Have each class design and make one or two sections of the quilt. Choose a theme such as harvest, Hallowe'en, or sports.

You can make your quilt a recycling project at the same time. Use scraps of old clothing to create your squares. Add buttons, felt, and colorful yarn to give your pictures extra texture. When the patches have been made, hold a series of quilting bees to sew the sections together. Hang your quilt in the hall for the whole school to enjoy!

Rag rugs

The first rugs used by the settlers were animal skins or furs that were thrown over dirt floors. In later times, the settlers made braided rugs from scraps of cloth and pieces of old clothing. The sturdy material of worn-out soldier's uniforms was ideal for making carpets.

Round and round

The rags were cut into strips that were about as wide as your thumb. These strips were sewn together at the ends to form a longer strip. Three long strips were braided to make a stronger strand. This strand was then sewn, as shown in the diagram in the margin, around and around itself until it formed a big, round or oval rug.

Woven mats

Settler families that owned looms were able to weave their rugs in the same way they wove their cloth. The warp threads on the loom were linen or heavy cotton. The strips of rags sewn together into long strands made up the weft threads and were wound around a large rag shuttle. The carpet that was woven on a loom was not very wide, but it could be made any length. By weaving many long sections and then sewing them together, the weaver could create a huge carpet. The settlers placed straw underneath the rug to make it feel warm and soft.

A rag rug for your room

Make a rag rug for your room or classroom. Collect old bits of material and braid them. Sew the braid in a circle, as shown in the diagram.

Sewing together a round rag rug

(opposite) As well as weaving cloth, settlers used their looms to weave rag rugs. Some weavers specialized in this task. Settlers brought their rags to the weaver, who wove them into rugs for a fee.

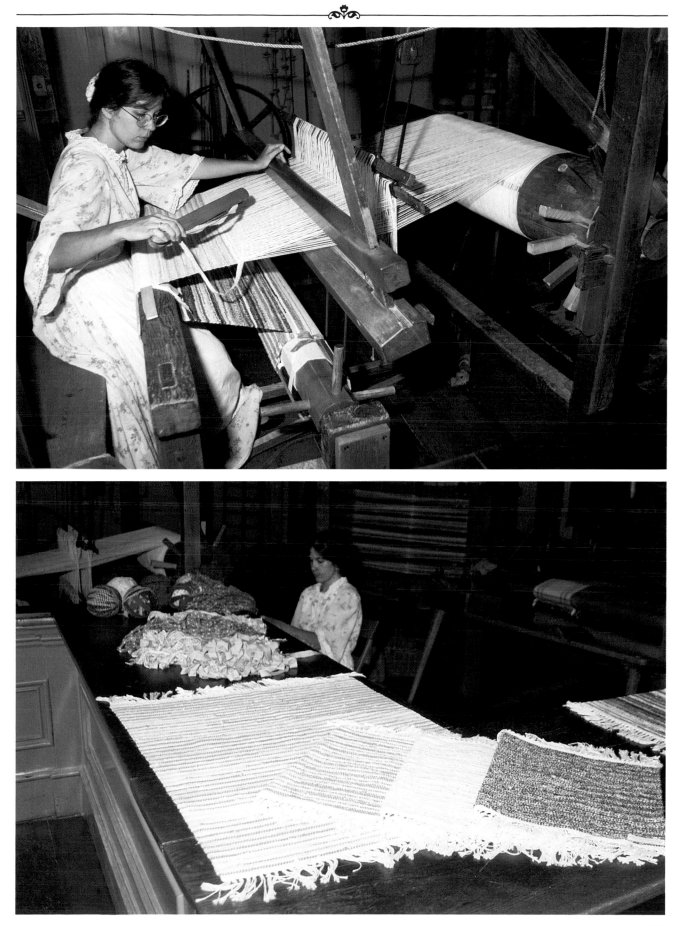

Leatherworkers made all sorts of items from leather. Everything from saddles to fine leather gloves began as animal skins.

Leather goods

Today we buy shoes in shoe stores. We have hundreds of choices of color and style. In the days of the very first settlers, most shoes were made in the home from animal hides. Many other things were made from animal hides, too, such as rugs, blankets, clothing, saddles, bags, flasks, buckets, and hats.

There were plenty of animals in the forests, so the settlers had no shortage of hides. Some hides were cleaned and used with the hair or fur still on them. Others were turned into leather by scraping off the fur, washing the hides, and then **tanning** them.

Tanning

Tanning is a soaking process that stops the skins of animals from decaying, preserves them, and turns them into leather. After a hide was cleaned, it was left to soak for three weeks in a chemical mixture made from water and ashes. A piece of **rawhide** was the result. This was kneaded and stretched by hand to make it soft. Then the rawhide was put into a tanning solution of hemlock and oak bark, where it was left to soak for about three months. The tanned leather was softened again by hand before it was ready to be made into shoes or clothes.

Drying was one way of preserving hides.

Many early settlers made their own shoes. These shoes fit on either foot and left plenty of room for heavy socks and growing feet.

Wood, straw, and feathers

The settlers used everything that was available to them. They were surrounded by trees, so there was plenty of wood for building homes and barns and for making furniture, tools, brooms, buckets, and barrels. It took a lot of chopping, sawing, and carving to turn wood into large and small objects for the home.

Straw

The settlers grew plants such as corn, oats, wheat, and rye. After the grain was removed, the rest of the plant was sometimes saved for later. Corn husks, for instance, were ideal for stuffing mattresses. Straw, the stalk of some plants, was used for making hats and floormats. It was woven into baskets and containers of all kinds. Straw was also used to make brooms.

Feathers

To provide them with meat, the settlers raised chickens, turkeys, ducks, and geese. Before these birds could be cooked, however, their feathers had to be plucked. Feathers were used in many different ways because they were soft and warm. Mattresses, couches, chairs, and pillows were stuffed with feathers to make them comfortable. **Down**, the soft underfeathers, were the warmest and softest of all.

(opposite) Here are two ways of making brooms. In the top picture, a broommaker ties straw together onto a wooden handle. In the bottom picture, a settler makes a wooden broom at home by carefully carving the end of the broom handle.

(below, left) Feathers kept the settlers warm just as they once kept the barnyard ducks and geese warm. Feathers were stuffed into bedding and the linings of jackets and coats.

(below, right) The settlers had only the simplest tools. Their creations were not smooth or refined, yet they had a handmade beauty all their own.

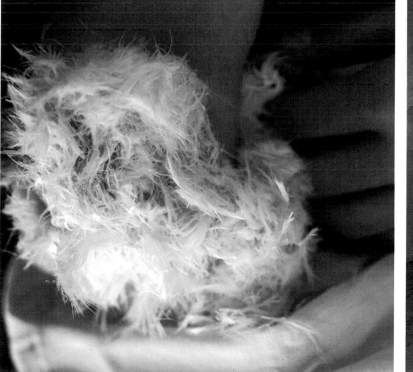

Sometimes a variety of ingredients were mixed into pioneer soap. For instance, ginger root, lavender, and bayberries were added to soap to give it a lovely scent.

Lye was made by packing ashes into a barrel. Hot water dripped through the ashes, producing a thick liquid.

Soap making

Settlers made soap from two main ingredients—**lye** and **tallow**. Both were easy to get at home. Lye comes from ashes. The settlers had plenty of ashes because they burned down parts of forests to make room for fields. Ashes were also collected from fireplaces.

Homemade lye

Lye is created when water drips through ashes. The settlers packed layers of straw and ashes into a barrel. The barrel, which had a slit at the bottom, was put on top of a raised platform. Hot water was poured into the barrel and trickled down through the ashes. A day later, a thick liquid acid, called lye, began to seep out of the hole and drip into a bucket or pot.

Melting fat

Tallow comes from melted fat. The process of melting fat is called **rendering**. Whenever the settlers butchered an animal, the leftover fat was used to make tallow. The settlers collected tallow in a wooden box or metal pot. They added used fat from their kitchens and kept it all until it was time to make soap or candles.

An outdoor job

Soap was made only once or twice a year. It was usually done outdoors because it was a messy, smelly job. Tallow and lye were boiled together over a fire in a big iron pot. Someone had to keep stirring constantly or the mixture would not blend properly. The thick mixture was poured into pans to harden. The cakes of soap were then cut into bars.

Tallow and lye were boiled in big iron pots.

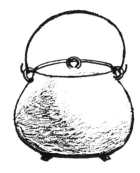

This woman has to be very careful as she makes soap. Lye is a very dangerous substance. If some splashes on her hands or arms, it will scorch her skin. If she gets too close and breathes in its fumes, it will burn her throat. Settler children were kept at a safe distance when soap was being made.

Dipping candles

You probably do not think about having light in your home until your electricity suddenly goes off one night in a thunderstorm. The settlers, on the other hand, did not take light for granted. When winter came, there were fewer hours of daylight, and the sun set early. In the evenings, the family sat huddled around the fireplace, but the room was still very dark. The settlers needed another source of light.

Making candles was not a pleasant chore, but it only had to be done once or twice each year.

Tallow and wax

As soon as they started raising farm animals, the settlers were able to make proper candles from tallow. Some tallow also came from the seeds of bayberries, which produced sweet-smelling candles that were saved for special occasions. Other candles were made from beeswax. Sometimes scents such as honey, pine, and ginger were added.

Where to get wicks

In order to work, candles need **wicks**. When you light a candle, you light the wick. When the wick burns, it pulls the wax towards it in order to use up the energy of this fuel. Wicks were made by spinning milkweed silk or fibers from the **hemp** plant. If the settlers lived in or near a village with a general store, they bought thick string to use as wicks.

Dip and harden

To make many candles at once, five or six wicks were tied to each of several sticks. The tallow and wax were melted in a huge pot, into which the wicks were dipped, one stick after another. After the tallow dried, the wicks were dipped again and again, adding more layers of tallow until the candles were the right thickness.

After each dipping, the candles had to be straightened because they curled at the ends. Thirty to fifty dippings later, the wicks were taken off the sticks, and another set was tied on. It took many hours to make enough candles to last a whole winter. The settlers were happy when they were finally able to buy candles in a shop.

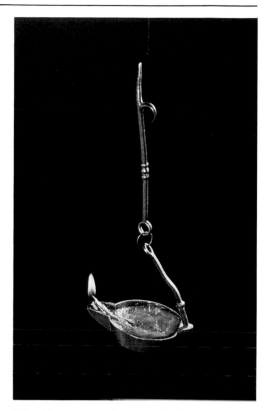

The first "candles," called Betty lamps, were nothing more than bowls of fat with a piece of rag in each, which served as a wick.

When the settlers could buy candle molds, making candles became less difficult. After tying a wick in place, tallow was poured into the molds and left to harden.

(top) *Today people have a renewed interest in learning the skills of making beautiful things by hand. Could you learn to make things from scratch if you had to? Which home craft would be your favorite?*

(bottom) *When machines such as this factory loom were invented, manufactured goods replaced home crafts.*

From home to factory

As communities grew into villages and then towns, more and more people needed goods made by professional craftspeople. These artisans took over much of the work that had been done in the home. Soon people invented machines to do the work that once took so long by hand. Factories began producing goods in large quantities. Life became much less difficult for the settlers when they could buy things ready-made.

When you visit an historic home, look at the furniture and objects. Most were made by hand. Watch the guides as they carry out their demonstrations. Learn to do a craft on your own. You can take pride in learning a very old skill and have fun at the same time!

Glossary

antique - At least one hundred years old

artisan - A skilled craftsperson

bayberry - A shrub that produces gray, waxy, sweet-smelling berries from which candles can be made

beater - The bar that tightens up the woven threads on a loom

bee - An event at which a group of volunteers performs a task

beeswax - The yellowish brown wax made by the honeybee that is found in honeycombs

carding - The combing of fibers to prepare them for spinning

crocheting - A kind of needlework using one hooked needle

early settler - A person who is among the first people to settle in an area. A settler from an early time in history. A pioneer

embroidery - The art of decorating fabric with fine needlework

ginger - An Asian plant whose root is used for flavoring or as a fragrance

ginning - The process of removing seeds from cotton fibers

goods - Items that are made to be sold

hemlock - An evergreen tree with short, flat needles, the bark of which is used for tanning leather

hemp - A tall plant whose stem contains fibers used for making string and rope

hide - The skin of an animal

historic - Important in history. Historic places are important in history because they teach us how the people who settled this continent lived in the past.

husk - The outer covering of grain

loom - A machine used for weaving cloth

mortar - A deep, hard bowl in which substances are ground

occupation - A job, trade, or profession

patchwork - Needlework which uses different colored patches of material

pestle - A bar with which substances are ground in a mortar

professional - A person who makes a living performing a highly skilled type of work

raw material - A material such as wood or iron from which things are made

rawhide - The untanned hide of animals

rug hooking - Making a rug by pulling yarn through coarse cloth

settler - A person who makes his or her home in a new country or part of a country that is not built up

shuttle - An instrument containing a spool of yarn that is passed back and forth between the warp threads on a loom. The shuttle carries the weft threads.

stalk - The stem of a plant

trade - A specialized way of earning a living

yarn - Any fiber, such as wool or flax, that has been spun into strands for weaving

Home crafts index

Acknowledgments

Photographs:
Marc Crabtree: Cover; p.7(top), 21(top and bottom)
Black Creek Pioneer Village/TRCA title page,
p.4(bottom), 6, 9(top), 11, 12, 13(top), 14(left and
right), 15(left and right), 16, 18(top), 24(top), 27, 28,
29(top and bottom), 30(top)
Jim Bryant: p.9(bottom), 25(right)
Sainte-Marie Among the Hurons: p.22, 23(top and
bottom)
Ken Faris: p.7(bottom), 13(bottom), 17, 18(bottom),
30(bottom)
Bob Mansour: p.4(top), 5, 8(bottom), 10, 24(bottom),
25(left), 26

Illustrations:
Cover: Antoinette "Cookie" DeBiasi
John Mantha: p.11, 12, 26
Greg Ruhl: p.19
David Willis: p.27

13 14 15 Printed in U.S.A.